DEAR WANDERING WILDEBEEST

And Other Poems from the Water Hole

Irene Latham

illustrated by Anna Wadham

MILLBROOK PRESS/MINNEAPOLIS

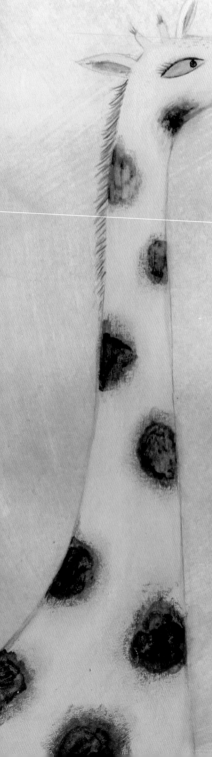

For Alex, Anna, BrenLeigh, JuliAnna,
Levi & Matt —I.L.

For Oscar —A.W.

Millbrook Press
A division of Lerner Publishing Group, Inc.
241 First Avenue North
Minneapolis, MN 55401 USA

For reading levels and more information, look up this title at
www.lernerbooks.com.

Main body text set in Gill Sans Infant Std 15/18. Typeface provided by Monotype Typography.

Library of Congress Cataloging-in-Publication Data

Latham, Irene.
    [Poems. Selections]
    Dear Wandering Wildebeest : And Other Poems from the Water Hole /
  By Irene Latham ; Illustrated by Anna Wadham.
        pages   cm
    ISBN 978–1–4677–1232–3 (lib. bdg. : alk. paper)
    ISBN 978–1–4677–4764–6 (eBook)
    I. Wadham, Anna, ill. II. Title.
  PS3612.A8685D43 2014
  811'.6—dc23   2013030195

Manufactured in the United States of America
1 – DP – 7/15/14

Contents

TO ALL THE beasts WHO ENTER here

Abandon now the crusted path
that resembles a human palm:

You
    are
        Here.

Welcome wildebeest
and beetle,

oxpecker and lion.
This water hole is yours.

It offers you oasis
beside its shrinking shores.

Drink, parched beasts.
Refresh and clean.

Discover this vital place
where earth and sky convene.

4

In the African grasslands, water holes are created during the rainy season when water collects in low-lying areas. Some water holes are deep and wide, and others are no bigger than a puddle. During the dry season, the water hole is the only source of water for miles around—while it lasts. Many grassland animals, such as giraffes, are able to go several days without water. But all the animals must drink to survive. That makes the water hole a busy place, and many different animals may gather together there at any given hour of the day.

Impala Explosion

Wind lifts
grass shifts

eyes search
legs lurch

twig pops
grazing stops

ears twitch
tails hitch

peace shatters
beasts scatter—

long leaps
athletic feats

flawless flight
dancer's delight.

Impalas are the picture of grace with their long, lean bodies and the curving, twisted horns of the males. When surprised or threatened, a herd of impalas will suddenly leap and jump, often over one another. These leaps can be as high as 8 feet (2.4 meters) and as long as 9 feet (2.7 m). Then, when the threat has passed, the impalas will resume drinking (or grazing), as if nothing ever happened. The animals' speed and agility is a prime defense against predators.

THE WATCHMAN'S SONG

Call me sentry,
call me guard.
I round the mounds
in the yard.

I stand up tall.
I scan the dirt.
I watch the town,
ears alert.

I sing my song:
peep peep peep.
It means, we're safe!
Forage! Sleep!

But if Jackal stalks
and closes in,
or if Hawk circles
yet again—

I'll *whistle-shrill.*
That means: Duck!
Grrrr-bark-rrrrr-bark.
Don't push luck!

Call me sentry,
call me guard.
I'm the keeper
of the yard.

Squirrel-sized animals called meerkats build their burrows close to the water hole. They are diurnal, which means they only come out during the daylight hours. They live in large cooperative groups called mobs, where they share jobs such as watchman and babysitter. Meerkats are famous for the way they stand up tall on their back legs, which makes them resemble tiny humans.

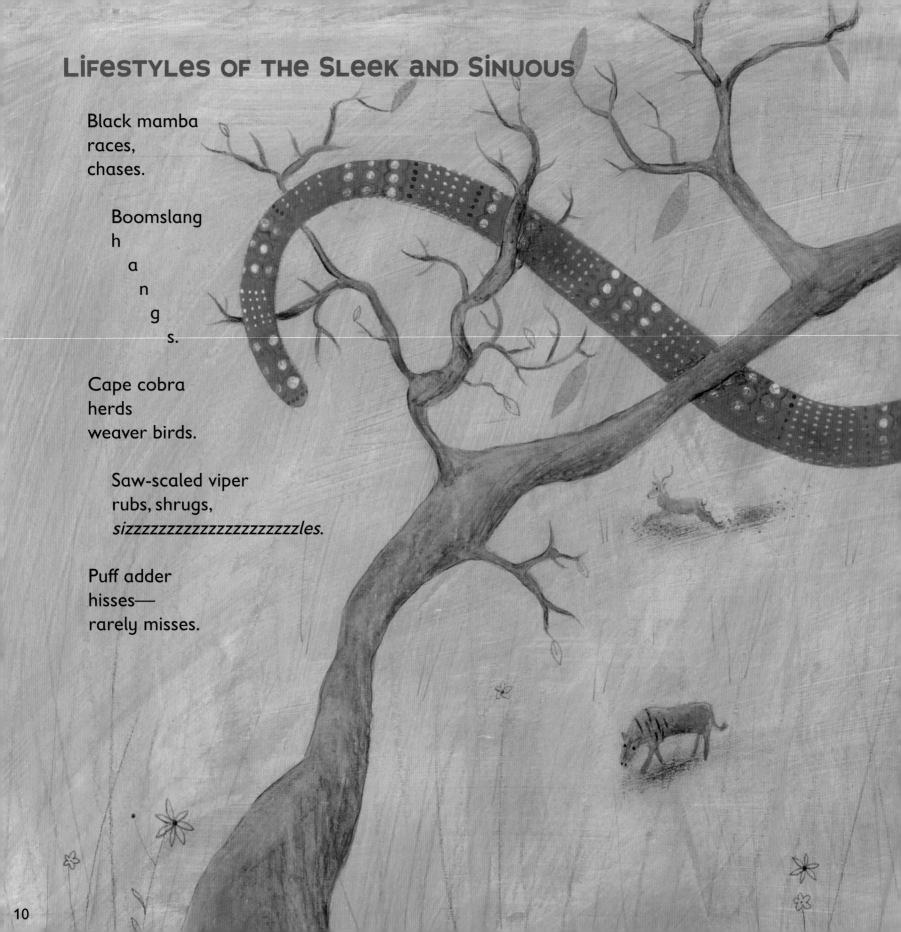

Lifestyles of the Sleek and Sinuous

Black mamba
races,
chases.

Boomslang
h
a
n
g
s.

Cape cobra
herds
weaver birds.

Saw-scaled viper
rubs, shrugs,
sizzzzzzzzzzzzzzzzzzzzles.

Puff adder
hisses—
rarely misses.

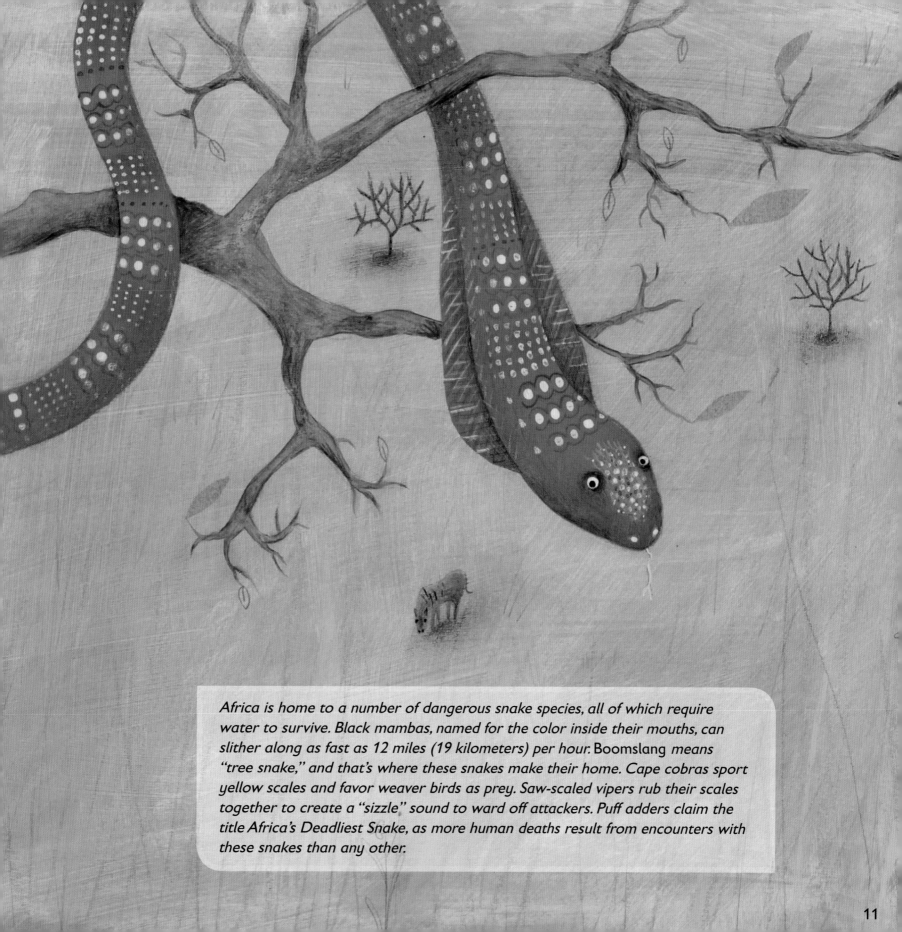

Africa is home to a number of dangerous snake species, all of which require water to survive. Black mambas, named for the color inside their mouths, can slither along as fast as 12 miles (19 kilometers) per hour. *Boomslang* means "tree snake," and that's where these snakes make their home. Cape cobras sport yellow scales and favor weaver birds as prey. Saw-scaled vipers rub their scales together to create a "sizzle" sound to ward off attackers. Puff adders claim the title Africa's Deadliest Snake, as more human deaths result from encounters with these snakes than any other.

Oxpecker Cleaning Service
Specializing in Large Beasts

Ticks got you dancing in an ear-flapping way?
Try our Basic Tick Removal Plan today!

We bring our own equipment (sharp claws and flattened beaks)
to comb, pick, and groom your hide until it shines and squeaks.

Got earwax? Dead skin? We're the best!
Deep wound cleaning upon request.

Trustworthy, dependable, professional crew
with years of experience bringing out the best *you.*

call 1-800-CLEAN ME
Clean is our guarantee!

Oxpeckers spend much of their lives perched on the backs, necks, or heads of large African mammals. The birds aren't there just to get a free ride to the water hole; it's how they feed themselves. Their survival depends on the abundance of insects and other edible bits they find hidden in the animals' coats. This arrangement benefits both bird and mammal.

TRIPTYCH FOR a THIRSTY GIRAFFE

I. Craving

Leaves turn
   to dust,
      mouth cottons,

tongue
   becomes
      swollen log.

Must find water.

II. Caution

Water hole, at last.

Rhinos, elephants,
warthogs, impalas.

Watch out for lions!

Security-camera eyes
scan water's edge.

Must be safe.

III. Courage

Long legs contort,
widen into triangles.

Step by step by step
      until, *yes!*

Tongue whirlpools water
into mouth.

Must not stop.

*The giraffe's long neck might be useful
for snatching leaves from high branches,
but it poses something of a problem at
the water hole. It can take a while for
giraffes to feel safe enough to perform the
acrobatics required to bend over and drink.
The awkward position of their legs while
drinking—and the time it takes for them to
get into and out of position—makes them
more vulnerable to predators.*

Stripes vs. Stripes

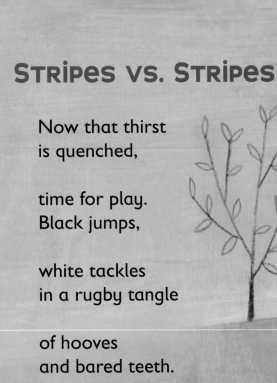

Now that thirst
is quenched,

time for play.
Black jumps,

white tackles
in a rugby tangle

of hooves
and bared teeth.

Whinny, snort,
kick, soar—

crowd roars!

Whole herd
scores.

After zebras have had their daily drink, they often hang around the water hole. They nibble one another's backs and sometimes race and kick out their legs. This playtime not only strengthens bonds within the herd but also protects the zebras. The fast-moving mass of stripes makes it difficult for predators to tell where one zebra ends and another begins.

DUNG BEETLE AT WORK

With hard-hat shell
and shovel claws,
Dung Beetle doesn't
ask for applause.

She rolls and scurries,
scurries and rolls—
no break, no water
till ball reaches hole.

African sun beams;
roller birds swoop.
Dung Beetle lays eggs
in elephant poop.

Eggs keep warm;
grass seeds grow.
Busy Dung Beetle's
a recycling pro!

A single elephant produces about 220 pounds (100 kilograms) of dung a day, some of which accumulates in piles around the water hole. Because elephants eat mainly grass, their dung contains a lot of grass seed. Before dung beetles get to work, butterflies drink up the moisture in the dung to dry it out. Beetles then roll what remains in small, compact balls, which they transport to their underground tunnels. The grass seeds begin to grow belowground, and the dung also offers a place for the beetles to lay their eggs. As beetle babies emerge, they seek out more dung, and the process continues.

tree for all

Giraffes feast on my leafy crown;
my buffet never closes.

Rhinos doze beneath my broad branches;
my umbrella shelters and shades.

Baboons scramble up and down my trunk;
my playground delights all ages.

Owls nest in my hidden knothole;
my cradle cozies brand-new wings.

Skinks sleep in my thick, spotted bark;
my camouflage keeps them safe.

Safari ants trail along my roots;
My roadways help build a city.

No grassland beast can resist my charms;
I am a wild bush willow tree.

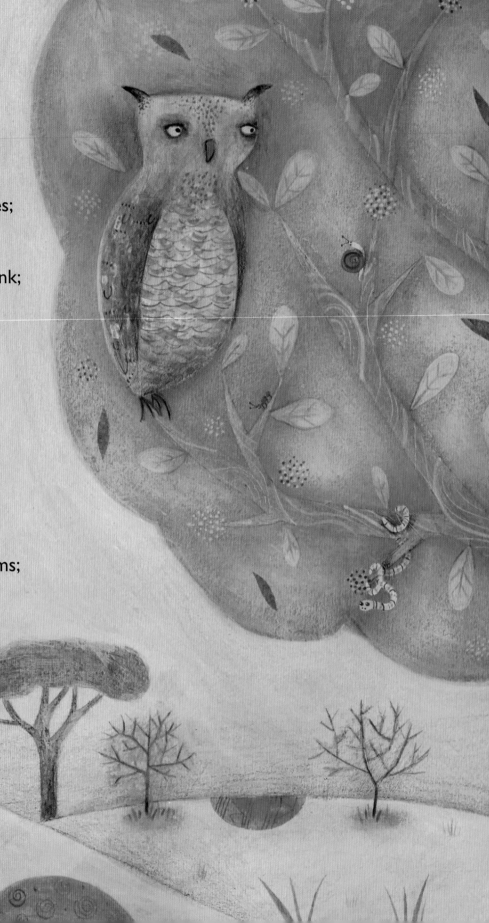

Bush willow, or Combretum, trees can often be found near a water hole. They have root systems that stretch deep underground so the trees can survive for a long time without rain. There are more than three hundred varieties of bush willow! Some take the form of a shrub. Others, like those on the savanna, can grow very large. This allows for many different types of animals to make use of the tree, whether for shade or feast or protection from predators.

Dear Wandering Wildebeest

Wander with me,
meander with me.

Come, be my companion
in this wildebeest sea.

We'll drink when we can,
stampede when we must.

We'll storm the savanna,
create waves of dust.

Come now, join the fray.

Let's graze away
the blazing days.

Let's embrace this season
of strife,

this shifting
        drifting
            life.

Herds of wildebeest travel great distances in search of grass and water. A member of the antelope family, these peculiar-looking animals are a favored prey for lions and other African cats. Once a year, usually in May or June, more than a million wildebeest migrate in search of better feeding grounds. They travel more than 800 miles (1,290 km) across the Serengeti Plain in east-central Africa. This is the largest mammal migration in the world. That's a lot of hooves stamping through the grasslands!

Calling Carcass Control

Wildebeest down:
weakling drowned
during migration!

Vultures volplane,
wings become weather vanes
for hungry hyenas.

Squabble ensues.
Whoops broadcast the news
to black-backed jackals.

Siren-howls
foul the air.
Vultures stick to task:

Tear and snatch,
latch and swallow—
until mean-eyed marabou arrives.

Bones stripped clean.
Scene soon rearranges;
water hardly ripples.

The water hole can be a dangerous place for young animals. Wildebeest calves sometimes misjudge the depth or breadth of the water and do not have the strength to pull themselves up the slick walls. But nothing is wasted in the grasslands. After the bones have been picked over by animals that prefer fresh meat, the scavengers arrive to polish off the remains. Within mere hours of its death, the prey will be reduced to a skeleton. Hyenas, jackals, and vultures all do their share, and the marabou stork takes care of the rest: its bald head is perfectly adapted for poking around a rotting carcass.

DUST BATH AT DUSK

Trunks become
dust hoses;
beasts strike poses

and preen in silhouette
created by the
hazy screen.

Soon skin
is powdered
in a red-grit shower

that banishes bugs
and becomes next day's
sunscreen.

One final
wallow,
one last trumpet—

all clean!

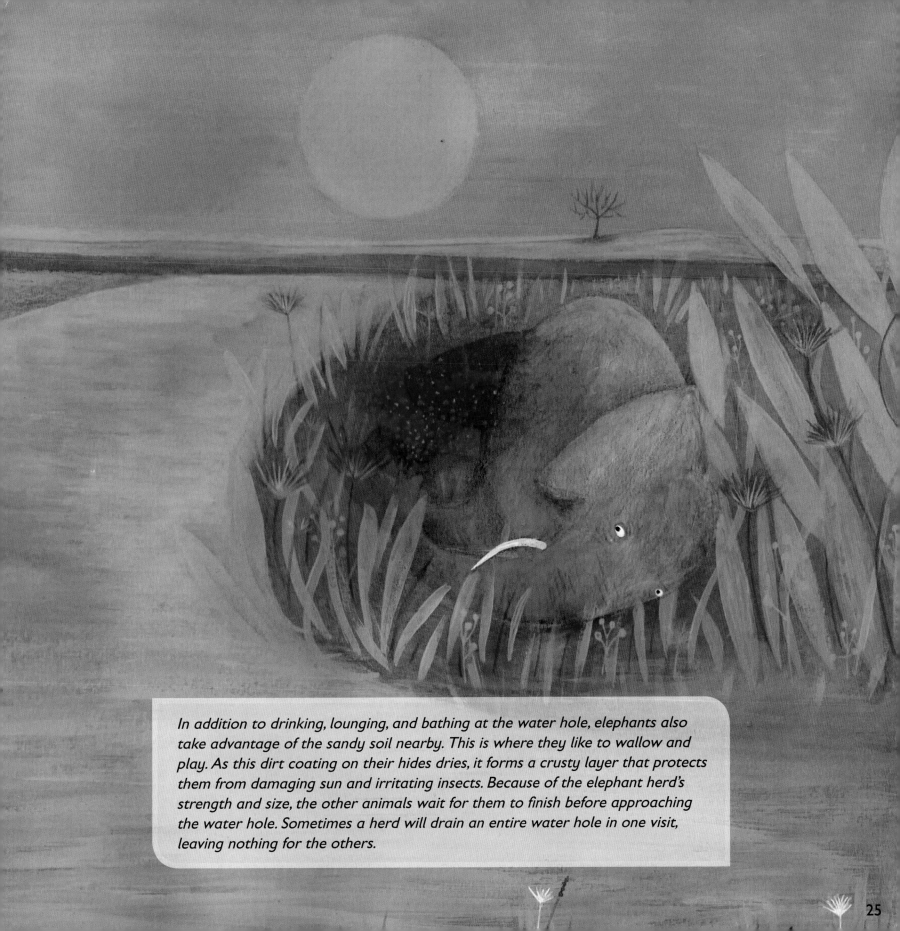

In addition to drinking, lounging, and bathing at the water hole, elephants also take advantage of the sandy soil nearby. This is where they like to wallow and play. As this dirt coating on their hides dries, it forms a crusty layer that protects them from damaging sun and irritating insects. Because of the elephant herd's strength and size, the other animals wait for them to finish before approaching the water hole. Sometimes a herd will drain an entire water hole in one visit, leaving nothing for the others.

What Rhino Knows

Rhino knows
to wait for starshine
and moonglow.

Rhino knows
to snort and paw,
puff and blow.

Rhino knows
to charge like a bull
at the rodeo.

Rhino knows
he's strong as
an armored buffalo.

Rhino knows
alone
is the only way to go.

26

The prehistoric-looking black rhinoceros may look like a tank with horns, but it suffers from a major shortcoming: poor eyesight. As a result, rhinos generally spend the daylight hours napping and only visit the water hole at night. These giant vegetarians are solitary by nature. When they meet one another at the water's edge, they defend their right to drink. Sometimes they charge. Other times they huff fiercely enough to raise clouds of dust. Occasionally they simply ignore one another.

Lioness, after the hunt

After the choosing,
after the chase,

after   rip
        claw
            tear—

after first taste.

Lioness lifts,
lopes

past rhino,
past antelope.

She crouches,
slouches,

savors favorite flavors,

and finally,
        finally
            dozes.

Lionesses are the hunters of the lion pride. After lions fill their bellies on wildebeest or other prey, the whole pride sleeps the hours away. They often visit the water hole after dark, lapping the water with their bumpy tongues in the same way a pet cat drinks from a bowl. Then they return to their favorite spots for more sleeping.

Says Nightjar to the Stars

Yes, I claim ground
and you call sky.

Your signature is a twinkle,
while mine is a *titititititit* sigh.

You peer down
while I'm looking up.

When I hear a stampede,
you call it a hiccup.

I'm the preacher
in a plain, somber suit;

you're the robed choir
wearing shiny black boots.

Come, let's join the beasts
in thanks and in praise—

sing a song for the water hole
that sustains us night and day.

The dark hours are busy at the water hole. Many animals, including nightjars, are frequent nighttime visitors. Nightjars are small birds—about the size of an adult human's palm—with drab gray coloring to help them blend in with their surroundings. They swipe insects as they fly past the water hole. The male nightjar's call is a startling sound that has the tendency to "jar" listeners, thus giving these birds the second part of their name.

Glossary

crown: the top or highest part of a tree

dung: animal waste (poop)

fray: argument or disagreement

oasis: a place in the desert where water can be found aboveground. More generally, a place that provides refreshing relief.

predator: an animal that hunts and eats other animals

prey: an animal hunted by another animal for food

pride: a group of lions

rugby: a type of ball game played by two opposing teams

savanna: a large, flat area with grass and few trees

sentry: one who stands guard

strife: fighting

triptych: a work of art divided into three sections

volplane: glide

FURTHER READING

Books

Callery, Sean. *Grassland.* New York: Kingfisher, 2012.
Learn about the grassland habitat, the life cycles of the animals that live there, and the food web that links them all together.

Catt, Thessaly. *Migrating with the Wildebeest.* New York: PowerKids Press, 2011.
We know that wildebeest wander. Want to get an in-depth look at the daily life of a migrating wildebeest? This book explains how the wet and dry seasons influence the wildebeest's patterns of migration.

Gangemi, Angelo. *Black Mamba.* New York: Gareth Stevens Publishing, 2011.
Do you want to know more about one of the world's deadliest snakes? This book will answer your questions about the black mamba's venom, diet, life cycle, and much more!

Joubert, Beverly, and Dereck Joubert. *Face to Face with Lions.* Washington, DC: National Geographic Children's Books, 2010.
This adventurous book introduces readers to the danger of life out on the African grasslands with up-close photographs of roaring, prowling lions. Have no fear, though—it also includes advice on "How Not to Get Eaten by a Lion"!

Latham, Donna. *Savannas and Grasslands.* White River Junction, VT: Nomad Press, 2011.
Learning about the dangerous animals that live on the savanna is exciting, but learning about how to protect these habitats is important too. This book lets you do both! Discover how you can help conserve this unique environment—and the animals that call it home.

Shalev, Zahavit. *Water Hole.* New York: DK Pub., 2005.
Spend twenty-four hours at a water hole and see the animals that come and go throughout the day in this photo-filled book.

Stone, Lynn M. *Zebras.* Minneapolis: Lerner Publications, 2009.
How do zebras confuse their enemies? Just how fast can a zebra run? These questions and more are answered in this exciting, photo-filled text.

Websites

African Wildlife—Animals
http://www.africaguide.com/wildlife/index.htm
This site offers information about African wildlife, including where to find each species and the latest on conservation efforts.

Animal Profiles—National Geographic
http://kids.nationalgeographic.com/kids/animals/
You'll find "creature features," videos, games, and more about animals from Africa (and other continents) at this site.

Photographer Captures Amazing Images of Lions After Submerging Himself in Watering Hole for Three Months
http://www.dailymail.co.uk/news/article-1253935/Photographer-captures-amazing-images-lions-watering-hole-submerging-months.html
See stunning wildlife photographs taken by Greg du Toit, who submerged himself in a Kenyan water hole. The photos also inspired the poems in this book.

Sounds of Africam * Birds
http://www.africam.com/wildlife/soundsafricambirds
Listen to sound recordings of African birdcalls, including the square-tailed nightjar.